A

NORMAN WARREN

A LION BOOK
Tring • Batavia • Sydney

Published by
Lion Publishing plc
Icknield Way, Tring, Herts, England
ISBN 0 7459 1449 7
Lion Publishing Corporation
1705 Hubbard Avenue, Batavia, Illinois 60510, USA
ISBN 0 7459 1449 7
Albatross Books Pty Ltd
PO Box 320, Sutherland, NSW 2232, Australia
ISBN 0 86760 973 7

First edition 1988

Acknowledgments
Photographs by Ikyrkans Internationella AV-Tjanst, page 14;
Lion Publishing: David Alexander, page 39,
David Townsend, pages 7, 10, 27, 34–35, 42 and cover (top and bottom right);
ZEFA (UK) Ltd, pages 22, 47 and cover (left)

Printed and bound in Thailand

CONTENTS

A certain faith   4

How do I know God loves me?   6

God's word, the Bible   9

God knows all about you   13

A new relationship   16

Chosen to belong to him   18

Adopted into his family   20

Accepted as you are   23

He forgives all your sins   26

I'm not perfect – why do I still sin?   30

The gift of the Holy Spirit   32

The body of Christ   36

Baptism into Christ   38

The Lord's Supper   41

The certainty of his coming   44

A certain future   46

A CERTAIN FAITH?

'There are so many millions of people, how can God possibly be interested in me?'

'I'm just a tiny cog in a huge machine – I don't matter.'

'God seems to be so far away. How can I know he loves me?'

'I hear people talking about God being with them. How can I know he is with me in my daily life?'

'I cannot even forgive myself, how can I know God forgives me?'

'The day of judgment, and death itself, fill me with fear.'

'How can I be sure death isn't the end?'

'How can I know there is life beyond the grave?'

'Will I go to heaven when I die?'

'You cannot be sure about anything anymore.'

These questions, and others like them, come to most people at one time or another. They can cause a lot of worry and unhappiness.

World events, the threat of nuclear explosions, the seeming silence and inactivity of God, all fill many with fear and uncertainty.

Others see the Bible being attacked, ridiculed and discredited, and ask themselves if they can trust it any longer.

Some feel that it is proud and presumptuous to say you can know God and have eternal life. Can we be really *sure*?

It is quite possible for you to believe in God, be baptized and even attend church, and yet not to be able to say definitely you are a Christian. Some days you feel you are, other days you just do not know. You try to live up to God's standards and hope all will turn out all right in the end, but you really don't know.

Deep down you long to have an inner certainty that you are forgiven and belong to God, and to know God's love in your life.

HOW DO I KNOW GOD LOVES ME?

Creation tells me that God loves me.

Just look around at the world that God has made. See the amazing beauty and colour, the care for detail, from the vastness of space and the wonder of the night sky to the restless sea, the soaring mountains to the gentleness of the hills and valleys, the design of a snowflake to the lumbering elephant, the intricacy of eye, ear and brain.

All this shows God's care for his world. We are part of his creation. He sends the sun and rain, he gives the fruitfulness of the earth, the riches of plant, insect and minerals, whether we acknowledge him or not.

The coming of Jesus tells me that God loves me.

I can get some idea of the Creator by studying creation, just as I can learn something of Bach by studying his music. But it all remains rather vague. God does reveal himself in his creation. But his perfect revelation came when he sent his Son Jesus Christ to be born into our world. That is the greatest proof of God's love.

> 'God loved the world so much that he gave
> his only Son so that everyone who believes
> in him may not die but have eternal life.'
> (John 3:16)

Jesus lived in a real place – in occupied Palestine – in real history, for about thirty-three years. The story is told from four different perspectives in the books we know as the Gospels, in the Bible.

As we see Jesus' loving acceptance of all people, no matter what their background, their intellect or their character, we see God's love in action. In his teaching he likened himself to a shepherd, the Good Shepherd, who knows his sheep by name, cares for them and is willing to die for them.

The Bible tells me that God loves me.

The Bible is full of God's love for all people. It is packed with promise after promise of how much God cares for us.

> God says, 'I have loved you with an
> everlasting love.'
> (Jeremiah 31:3)

In the book of Hosea, there is a beautiful, intimate picture of God's love even for those who do not acknowledge it.

> 'I took my people up in my arms,
> I drew them to me with affection and love,
> I picked them up and held them to my cheek;
> I bent down to them and fed them.'
> (Hosea 11:3-4)

GOD'S WORD, THE BIBLE

Can I really trust the Bible? Is it true?

The word Bible comes from a Greek word *biblia* which means 'books'. The Bible is not one book but sixty-six books. It took about 1,500 years to be completed and was written by about forty people. Among them were kings, a prime minister, a doctor, a tax official, fishermen and a farmer. Most of the writers never met the other writers. Yet through the Bible there runs an amazing unity and agreement. What is the explanation?

God spoke through the Bible's writers. Through their personalities, their different styles, through their actual words he guided them to write down *his* words. They did not just sit down and write a book about God. Again and again we have the words, 'Thus says the Lord', or 'The word of the Lord came to . . .' The apostle Peter put it like this:

> 'No prophetic message ever came just from
> the will of man, but men were under the
> control of the Holy Spirit as they spoke the
> message that came from God.'
> (2 Peter 1:21)

Paul summed it up:

> 'All scripture is inspired of God.'
> (2 Timothy 3:16)

The Bible tells us what God is like, and how we can know him. Without it we would know next to nothing

about him. We would have no idea why we are here or where we are going.

The Bible is packed full of God's promises to his people.

The trouble with some people is that they do not read their Bible to find out these promises. Instead of relying on God's word, they rely on their own feelings or ideas. If you are tired or ill, if you have troubles and worries at home or at work, you may not feel God is with you and loves you. Don't rely on your feelings which change.

Let the Bible be your guide through life.

> 'Your word is a lamp to my feet and a light
> to my path.'
> (Psalm 119:105)

Let the Bible keep you from sin.

> 'I have hidden your word in my heart that I
> might not sin against you.'
> (Psalm 119:11)

Let the Bible strengthen your faith.

> 'Faith comes from hearing the message and
> the message is heard through the word of
> God.'
> (Romans 10:17)

The Bible sheds light on all our problems. It speaks with certainty on life, death and eternity. It is our guidebook from earth to heaven.

Let the Bible build you up in the Christian life.

> 'Now I commit you to God and to the word
> of his grace which can build you up.'
> (Acts 20:32)

Let the Bible give you a confident faith.

> 'I write these things to you who believe in
> the name of the Son of God so that you may
> know that you have eternal life.'
> (1 John 5:13)

GOD KNOWS ALL ABOUT YOU

'There are so many people in the world, how can God possibly love me.'

We sometimes have a picture of God rather like a harrassed telephone operator, desperately trying to connect all the calls that are flooding in. God is not a very big human. He is far, far greater than our tiny, finite minds can ever take in. He has perfect knowledge of everything, of everyone. He knows all about you. The psalmist recognized this in one of the most beautiful of all Psalms:

> 'Lord you have examined me and you know
> me.
> You know everything I do; from far away,
> you understand all my thoughts.
> You see me whether I am working or
> resting; you know all my actions.
> Even before I speak you already know what
> I will say.
> You are all around me on every side; you
> protect me with your power.
> Your knowledge of me is too deep; it is
> beyond my understanding.
> You created every part of me; you put me
> together in my mother's womb;
> when I was growing there in secret, you
> knew that I was there.'
> (Psalm 139:1-6,13,15)

God knows us as no one else does or can. And he loves us.

We see from the life of Jesus, too, God's care for and interest in the individual. Jesus was always ready to spare time with a person, no matter who they were nor what they had done – a proud Pharisee, an immoral woman, lepers and outcasts, sad and lonely people, ordinary people – he accepted them all.

He is interested in us as individuals. We are of infinite worth to him, so much that he was prepared to die for us. That is how much value we are to him. He knows everything about us, the worst as well as the best, and loves us just the same.

'I have called you by name – you are mine
. . . you are precious to me, I love you and
give you honour.'
(Isaiah 43:1,4)

A NEW RELATIONSHIP

A Christian is not someone who just does religious things. Going to church no more makes you a Christian than going to the zoo makes you a chimpanzee.

A Christian is someone who belongs to Jesus Christ; Christ's man, Christ's woman. A Devonian is someone who loves Devon and who belongs there. So a Christian is someone who loves Christ, who belongs to Christ, someone who has let the living Christ enter his or her life to be Lord. For Jesus not only lived in real history. He died, too – and was raised from death to new life.

Some years ago I visited a refugee camp in South Austria. All the year round people were streaming over the Yugoslav frontier into Austria. I remember a young Hungarian woman who had watched her parents die of starvation. She decided to make a break for freedom. She crossed at the Austrian frontier and was given a visa stamped with the exact time and place she entered her new country.

I met a young Russian who determined to leave the horrors of Communist oppression. His escape through Poland, Czechoslovakia and Yugoslavia was a thriller. Finally he crossed the Karavanken mountains into the freedom of Austria. He did not know when he crossed the frontier, he just kept pressing on until he reached an Austrian village and safety.

These two people had this in common; they knew they were free, they were in a new country with a new language to learn, new friends to make and a new government to obey. All was not going to be easy, but they knew they were free.

In the same way, tired of the dictatorship of sin and disillusioned by the emptiness of life, we long for a new life. We acknowledge our sin, we 'repent', we turn our back on it. We commit our life to Jesus Christ, we ask him to take over our life.

Some know the exact moment they crossed the frontier to this new life. Some cannot be sure of the precise moment or day. The important thing is not when, but that you know now.

For the Christian the new country is the kingdom of God. For the Christian the new government is the rule of Christ. This is how the apostle Paul put it:

> 'When anyone is joined to Christ, he is a
> new being; the old is gone, the new has come.'
> (2 Corinthians 5:17)

Have you put your trust in Jesus? Have you accepted him into your life as Lord? Then you are in his kingdom, in his care. You are a Christian. You belong to him for eternity.

CHOSEN TO BELONG TO HIM

The trouble with many Christians is that they think it
all depends on them. They hear the good news of Jesus
and accept him – they decide for Jesus. It's their choice,
their decision. Nothing could be further from the truth.
It is God's doing. Faith is depending on *him*, not on
ourselves. God makes all the moves. Long before you
were born he knew all about you. Years before you ever
gave God a thought he knew you and chose you to
belong. This is something we find so hard to grasp. St
Paul put it like this:

> 'Even before the world was made, God had
> already chosen us to be his through our
> union with Christ, so that we would be holy
> and without fault before him. Because of
> his love God had already decided that
> through Jesus Christ he would make us his
> sons [and daughters!].'
> (Ephesians 1:4-5)

He knew you would respond to his love. His Holy Spirit
had been at work in you even before your birth, leading
you closer to Christ. We are not robots. God does not
force anyone to believe. He honours our will, for that is
what makes us human beings, with the ability to
choose.

Jesus likened himself to a shepherd going after the lost
sheep until he found it. It is only as we look back over
our life that we can see how wonderfully God has been

at work – guiding and protecting us, sending *that* person at *that* moment to be God's messenger, putting *that* book into our hands, causing us to go and hear *that* speaker, even allowing a seeming tragedy to happen that made us to turn to him for help.

Jesus summed it up so simply:

> 'You did not choose me, I chose you.'
> (John 15:16)

The emphasis is on him choosing us; we respond to his love. It brings home to us that our salvation is all of his love and grace and totally undeserved on our part. It destroys all our pride as we realize it is all his doing.

As we grasp this, just how precious each Christian is to Christ, it gives a great inner peace, and an assurance that he will most certainly look after his own.

> 'My sheep listen to my voice; I know them
> and they follow me. I give them eternal life
> and they shall never die. No one can snatch
> them away from me.'
> (John 10:27-28)

ADOPTED INTO HIS FAMILY

One of our children is adopted. He was born in Saigon in Vietnam towards the end of the war. He was left at an orphanage door with no name, no known parentage – just wrapped up in a piece of cloth.

He was chosen by us, set apart for us, given our name and after eighteen months legally adopted into our family. He didn't know what was going on, he was too young and confused. He was loved and accepted long before he could make any response. He has exactly the same rights as our other children, an heir to all we have. There is absolutely no difference in any way in his status and relationship in our family from the natural children.

This picture of adoption is used in the Bible to show the status of the Christians in God's family.

> 'The Spirit makes you God's children
> (literally, you have received the spirit of
> adoption) and by God's Spirit we cry out to
> God, "Father! My Father!"'
> (Romans 8:15)

Paul uses for 'father' the intimate word 'Daddy! My Daddy!'

By trusting in Jesus we become not just children in his family, but legally recognized heirs as well.

Jesus is the son and heir. We too become joint heirs with him, and will possess all the blessings and rights and inheritance that he keeps for his people. 'It is the Father's will to give you the kingdom,' said Jesus. Long before we knew anything about Christ, long before we responded, his love was upon us, we were chosen and set apart to belong in his family and to share with Christ the glorious inheritance that belongs to all the children of God. Princes and princesses of God's kingdom – that is what we are in Christ!

Peter was so excited by the prospect that he wrote,

> 'Let us give thanks to the God and Father
> of our Lord Jesus Christ. Because of his
> great mercy he gave us new life by raising
> Christ from death. This fills us with a
> living hope and so we look forward to
> possessing the rich blessings that God keeps
> for his people. He keeps them for you in
> heaven, where they cannot decay or spoil or
> fade away. They are for you who are kept
> safe by God's power for the salvation which
> is ready to be revealed at the end of time.'
> (1 Peter 1:3-5)

Look through these verses again and mark the promises. Turn them into a prayer of praise and thanksgiving.

ACCEPTED AS YOU ARE

This is the cornerstone of the Christian faith. You do not have to become good before God accepts you. If that were so, none of us would ever be Christians. He accepts us not because of anything in us, anything we have done, but only because of Jesus – who he is and what he has done for us. If it all depended upon us we would for ever be full of doubts. Because it all depends upon him we can be absolutely certain that we are fully accepted into his family.

A man called Martin Luther discovered this way back in the sixteenth century. He longed for peace with God. To find it he tried everything the church could offer – penances, priesthood, endless prayers, long pilgrimages. He still could not find peace. In fact he became more guilt-ridden and depressed.

It was when he was studying Paul's letter to the Romans that light dawned on him. He had already seen Christ's suffering in the Psalms: 'My God, my God, why have you forsaken me?' Martin, too, felt this deep separation from God. But then in Romans he saw that Christ's suffering and death were for human sin – *his*. Christ had died for Martin's sin.

It makes no difference who we are, or even what we are like. God is able to welcome us as friends.

Jesus took the full weight of God's holy anger towards sin in our place. God declares us, the guilty sinners, 'just', because Jesus, the innocent one, out of pure love suffered the consequences of our sin. We are justified in God's sight by faith in Christ and his death for us: justified – just-as-if-I-died.

Jesus died in my place, for my sin. For Martin Luther, this was a fresh discovery. As he grasped this and put his whole trust in his Saviour Jesus, he wrote, 'I felt myself to be re-born and to have gone through open doors into paradise. The whole of Scripture took on a new meaning. Whereas "the justice of God" had filled me with hate, now it became to me inexpressibly sweet in greater love.'

Jesus was cut off from his Father so that we might enter into his love. He was rejected that we might be accepted. He took our sin and guilt that we might be forgiven. He died that we might live. If God himself declares us acquitted from all our guilt, how dare we question it? When God's word tells me this, how can I question it?

When God sees me, he now sees Christ in me. How can I doubt? I can only accept it gladly, humbly and thankfully. This is how Paul sums it up:

> 'If God be for us, who can be against us? Certainly not God who did not even keep back his own Son, but offered him for us all! He gave us his Son – will he not also freely give us all things?
> Who will accuse God's chosen people? God himself declares them not guilty. Who, then, will condemn them? Not Christ

Jesus, who died, or rather who was raised to life and is at the right-hand side of God, pleading with him for us.

Who can separate us from the love of Christ? Can trouble do it, or hardship or persecution or hunger or poverty or danger or death? I am certain that nothing can separate us from his love: neither death nor life, neither angels nor other heavenly rulers or powers, neither the present nor the future, neither the world above nor the world below – there is nothing in all creation that will ever be able to separate us from the love of God which is ours through Christ Jesus our Lord.'

(Romans 8:31-39)

HE FORGIVES YOU ALL YOUR SINS

One of the results of sin is to cut us off from God. It is our doing, not God's. Nothing evil can exist in his presence, any more than darkness can co-exist with light. This is why he seems distant and unreal, and not concerned with our frustrations and worries. This is why it seems as if our prayers get no further than the ceiling.

The trouble with many Christians is that they go on thinking they can bridge the gap by their own efforts, by their religious activities and good works, hoping they are doing enough to please God. But of course they can never be sure they have ever done enough to earn God's approval and forgiveness.

Jesus' death on the cross tells us that God loves us, accepts us as we are and forgives our sins as we put our trust in him. Jesus bore the full consequences of all human sin,

> 'For Christ died for sins once and for all, a good man on behalf of sinners, in order to lead you to God.'
> (1 Peter 3:18)

We can never reach perfection for our sin destroys the pattern of our lives.

Forgiveness of our sins rests entirely on the finished work of Jesus on the cross. Just before he died Jesus cried out in a loud voice,

> 'It is finished.'
> (John 19:30)

This was a shout of victory – 'The work is done! The debt of man's sin is paid, finished, blotted out for ever.' We can never earn forgiveness. The Bible tells us that even our good works are like filthy rags compared to the absolute perfection of God.

The cross tells us that the enormous debt of our sin has been fully paid by Jesus Christ once and for all. When we accept Jesus into our lives, we receive God's forgiveness. Every sin we have ever done is blotted out for ever.

> 'As far as the east is from the west, so far does he remove our sins from us.'
> (Psalm 103:12)

God is able not only to forgive all our sins but to forget them, totally blot out of his memory all knowledge of them.

> 'I will forgive their sins and I will no longer remember their wrongs.'
> (Jeremiah 31:34)

You may well find this hard to understand and accept, but this is the measure of God's love for you.

One of the most beautiful illustrations of God's love and forgiveness is shown in Jesus' parable of the Prodigal Son. The younger son wants his father's money to live his life his own way. He wastes the lot and when left with nothing he remembers his father and determines to go home expecting to be disowned and punished. He is truly sorry. 'I have sinned against God and against you. I am no longer fit to be called your son.' But the father wraps his arms around him, gives him new clothes and a ring, the sign of his sonship. There is not one word of rebuke – just total acceptance and forgiveness.

Paul sums it up in these words:

> 'Let us praise God for his glorious grace,
> for the free gift he gave us in his dear Son.
> For by the death of Christ we are set free,
> that is, our sins are forgiven.'
> (Ephesians 1:7)

I'M NOT PERFECT – WHY DO I STILL SIN?

When we ask Jesus Christ into our lives we become a son or daughter of God. We have begun a new life. We have been born again. God the Father fully accepts us and forgives us for Jesus' sake. He becomes our Father; we become his child. A new relationship between us and him has been established that nothing can break.

This does not mean we suddenly become perfect. A criminal who has served his prison sentence is, in the eyes of the law, a free man. But he doesn't suddenly become perfect. He is the same person inside. But with the Christian there is a big difference. God gives us the Holy Spirit. Our aim now is not to please ourselves, but to please Jesus and to live for him and to become like him.

God has given us the Holy Spirit to do this work in us. But sadly we still sin, however hard we try. God has given us a new nature, but the old one will be with us until the day we die when it will be removed from us for ever.

What happens if I sin? Do I have to ask Jesus into my life all over again? Will God reject me or disown me?

Imagine a boy playing football in the garden who kicks the ball right through a window and smashes it. He had been told not to play there with the football. He keeps out of the way. At mealtime there is an icy silence, for he knows he has disobeyed his father. This will last until he owns up and says he is sorry. The relationship has not changed; he is still a son; he doesn't have to ask to become a member of the family. He never ceases to be a son. It is the friendship that has been temporarily broken, until he says he is sorry.

When you disobey Christ, or are thoughtless or self-centred, when you do, say or think something you know to be wrong, you are still a child of God. He doesn't disown you. The relationship has not changed – you do not have to be born again into God's family. You are in his family. You do not have to ask Jesus into your life again. He is already there. What you have done is to spoil the friendship with him, and it is up to you to own up and say sorry and ask for his forgiveness. This is how the apostle John put it:

> 'If we say we have no sin, we deceive
> ourselves and there is no truth in us. But if
> we confess our sins to God, he will keep his
> promise and do what is right: he will
> forgive us our sins and purify us from all
> our wrongdoing.'
> (1 John 1:8-9)

THE GIFT OF THE HOLY SPIRIT

When you receive Jesus into your life you receive the Holy Spirit. You cannot be a Christian without having the Holy Spirit. He is Jesus' personal representative in your life. Jesus' resurrection body is in heaven where he is at the place of all power and authority. While on earth he could only be at one place at a time. By sending the Holy Spirit he can be with all Christians at all times and in all places. He promised,

> 'I am with you always to the end of the
> age.'
> (Matthew 28:20)

He has kept his promise by sending the Holy Spirit. His special work in the Christian is to assure us of God's love and to empower us in our service and witness.

He assures us that the gospel is true.

> 'The Helper will come – the Spirit, who
> reveals the truth about God.'
> (John 15:26)

He assures us that we really are in Christ.

> 'We are sure that we live in union with God
> and that he lives in union with us, because
> he has given us his Spirit.'
> (1 John 4:13)

He assures us that God is our Father.

> 'For the Spirit that God has given you does

not make you slaves or cause you to be
afraid; instead the Spirit makes you God's
children and by the Spirit's power we cry
out to God, "Father! My Father!"'
(Romans 8:15)

He assures us that we truly belong to God.

'Do not make God's Spirit sad, for the
Spirit is God's mark of ownership on you.'
(Ephesians 4:30)

He assures us we are special in God's sight.

'God has poured his love into our hearts by
means of the Holy Spirit who is God's gift
to us.'
(Romans 5:5)

'Your body is the temple of the Holy Spirit
who lives in you.'
(1 Corinthians 6:19)

When doubts come, remind yourself:

- who you are: a sinner, yes, but saved by Christ.
- who you belong to: the Lord Jesus Christ, Lord of heaven and earth.
- who you have in you: God's Holy Spirit.
- what you are part of: the body of Christ, the church.

It is exhilarating to feel the power of wind and sea. The Bible speaks of the Holy Spirit as the 'breath of God' and the 'water of life'. ⟶

THE BODY OF CHRIST

It is quite true that as an individual you give your life to Christ. You personally trust in him as your Saviour and Lord. But you are not meant to be a kind of Robinson Crusoe, living on your own and having to rely on your own resourcefulness. When you trust in Christ you become one with him, the head. But you also become one with his body; the church.

The church is not a building, it is not bricks and mortar and glass, pews and organs. It is *people*, ordinary people from all countries and backgrounds, of all races, tribes and languages, all cultures, colours and classes who have this in common – they love Jesus and follow him. The church is described in many ways in the Bible: God's own people, a holy nation, the army of God, the family of God, the flock of Christ, God's temple, the bride of Christ.

Perhaps the picture of the body is the most vivid one, the body of Christ. The church is permanently and perfectly joined to Christ the head, who directs and controls the whole body. (See 1 Corinthians 12.) Not only are you as a Christian linked inseparably to Christ, and the Holy Spirit like the life-blood flows into you and through you. You are also joined to the other members.

Just as in a human body there are many parts, so also in Christ's body. We are all different. We each have a particular function. No one member is more important than the other. We each need each other if the body is to function properly. If one is hurting we all feel it and share it. Each is of infinite value, each has his or her own contribution and gifts.

It is this church against which, Jesus said, the gates of hell cannot prevail. It is this church, Paul said, that is loved by Christ, who gave his life for it to dedicate it and cleanse it, in order to present it to himself in all its beauty – pure and spotless.

It is this church that is commissioned to proclaim the good news of Jesus to all people and make disciples.

It is this church that will be gathered from every part of the world at Christ's return, with not one member missing, to reign and live with him in glory in heaven, gathering together all those still living and all those who have died in faith.

Make sure you are an active, committed member of the body of Christ where you live: join a local church where the gospel is loved and preached, so that you may 'grow up in every way to Christ, who is the head.'

BAPTISM INTO CHRIST

Baptism is the sign or mark of the Christian faith. Being baptized no more makes someone a Christian than a ring makes someone married. The ring in marriage is the symbol that a couple *are* married. The man and the woman have made solemn promises to each other, a covenant between them has been made and the ring is the outward sign of this. Baptism is the outward sign that you have pledged your life to Jesus. It is the public acknowledgment that you have turned from your old way of life and put your trust in Jesus as your Lord and Saviour.

It gives to the Christian great assurance that he or she is Christ's. In baptism you are acknowledging that Jesus is Lord. It is the public testimony that you belong to him. It marks your entrance into the family of God. It is the outward sign that you have been born again, that you are a child of God, a member of his body.

> 'All of us have been baptized into the one
> body by the same Spirit.'
> (1 Corinthians 12:13)

Baptism is like a visual aid of the gospel. It portrays Jesus' death and resurrection and shows the Christian's oneness with his Lord.

> 'When we were baptized into Christ we
> were baptized into his death so that as
> Christ was raised from death by the

At the start of his ministry Jesus was baptised in the River Jordan. He did not need to wash away any sin of his own, but wanted to identify with the failures of others.

> glorious power of the Father so also we
> might live a new life.'
> (Romans 6:3-4)

Baptism is like a symbolic burial of your old life, an end to the life of self. It is also the symbol of your new life in Christ, sharing his resurrection life. The apostle Paul put it so clearly:

> 'I have been put to death with Christ on the
> cross, so that it is no longer I who live, but
> it is Christ who lives in me.'
> (Galatians 2:20)

Baptism is a picture that every Christian has been cleansed from sin through Christ's death.

> 'So let us come near to God with a sincere heart and a sure faith, with hearts that have been purified from a guilty conscience and with bodies washed with pure water.'
> (Hebrews 10:22)

Baptism is a constant reminder of your new life in Christ and his gift of the Holy Spirit to dwell in you.

Baptism is the sign of your willingness to present your body to God as an instrument for his will and service.

Baptism is the signing on in the King's army, it is a declaration of war against sin and evil and the devil.

THE LORD'S SUPPER

The first Lord's Supper took place on the last Thursday of Jesus' earthly life, just before Good Friday and his death on the cross. He met with his disciples to celebrate the Jewish Passover. This reminded the Jews of their amazing escape from slavery in Egypt centuries earlier. God's Angel of Death was going to destroy all the first-born in the land. The Jews were told to sprinkle the blood of a perfect lamb over the doorposts of their houses and the angel would 'pass over' them.

Jesus gave this family meal, this Passover, a new and deeper meaning. He was the perfect lamb to be slain, his blood was to be sprinkled on the cross, so that God's judgment would pass over all who trust in him. This is how Paul describes it:

> 'For I received from the Lord the teaching
> that I passed on to you: that the Lord
> Jesus, on the night that he was betrayed,
> took a piece of bread, gave thanks to God,
> broke it and said, "This is my body which
> is given for you. Do this in memory of
> me."'
> (1 Corinthians 11:23-25)

The Lord's Supper proclaims the Lord's death by words and symbols. Christ's body is represented by the bread, his blood by the wine. The bread is broken and the wine poured out as a visual aid of Jesus' death on the cross. It is also called the Breaking of the Bread or Holy Communion to show our oneness with Jesus and with our fellow-Christians. It is sometimes called the

We share mealtimes with families and friends. The bread and wine of the Lord's Supper remind us of our friendship with God through Jesus.

Eucharist, a Greek word meaning 'thanksgiving', because Jesus gave thanks when he took the bread and cup of wine. It is a memorial meal, to remind Christians of the centre of our faith – the cross. As we share in it we are sharing in Christ's death. It expresses our oneness with Christ and with our fellow-Christians as we share the bread and wine.

It assures us of his love in dying for us. It strengthens our faith as we see the symbols of his love before our eyes. We feed upon him by faith. Jesus said:

> 'I am the bread of life. He who comes to
> me will never be hungry. He who believes
> in me will never be thirsty.'
> (John 6:35)

The Lord's Supper looks ahead to the second coming of Jesus in glory, something to fill us with joy and hope and praise.

> 'Every time you eat the bread and drink
> from this cup you proclaim the Lord's
> death until he comes.'
> (1 Corinthians 11:26)

THE CERTAINTY OF HIS COMING

'As I look out at the world I sometimes get really afraid.'

'Will we blow ourselves up? How is it all going to end?'

'Is God really in control? How can I be sure?'

'Will I go to heaven when I die?'

The Bible tells us on page after page that God is the sovereign Lord of heaven and earth.

> 'The Lord is King. He is clothed with
> majesty and power. The Lord rules
> supreme in heaven.'
> (Psalm 93:1,4)

Jesus said:

> 'I have been given all authority in heaven
> and on earth.'
> (Matthew 28:18)

God's purpose for his world is slowly but surely being worked out. Evil is still rampant, but the day is fast coming when,

> 'In honour of the name of Jesus all beings
> in heaven, on earth and in the world below
> will fall on their knees and all will openly
> proclaim that Jesus is Lord to the glory of
> God the Father.'
> (Philippians 2:10)

Jesus won the victory on the cross once and for all. The devil, called Satan in the Bible as the very personification of evil, is a defeated foe, his time is short. The final destruction of all evil will be when Jesus comes again. His promise is sure,

> 'I will come again and take you to myself,
> so that you will be where I am.'
> (John 14:3)

The New Testament is full of the certainty of Jesus' return in glory to end human history, to stop evil once and for all, to gather all his people into the heavenly kingdom he is preparing for them.

> 'So we shall always be with the Lord.'
> (1 Thessalonians 4:17)

Until that day there will be wars and suffering. God allows us our freedom of choice and it is this that is the cause of the crime and evil and subsequent suffering. But God is active in his world. His grace and love are constantly calling people to turn to him and trust him. He is with his people in their pain and hurts. No suffering, no trouble of any kind can ever separate us from his love. (Read again Paul's triumphant words in Romans 8:35-39. See page 25.)

A CERTAIN FUTURE

Illness and physical pain, tragedies, accidents and death will come to Christians as to others, simply because we are human. We will suffer because of other people's greed and selfishness, because we are part of society and what we do affects others for good and bad.

But God promises us a new body when we die, a resurrection body like Jesus' body. Just as a bird has a body for flying in the sky, the fish a body for living in the sea, and we have a body for living on earth, so when we die we shall be given a body just right for living in heaven. The apostle John wrote,

> 'We know that when Christ appears we
> shall be like him, because we shall see him
> as he really is.'
> (1 John 3:2)

> 'Thanks be to God who gives us the victory
> through our Lord Jesus Christ.'
> (1 Corinthians 15:57)

The Christian can face the world, life and all it throws at us, the future, even death itself, with total confidence – not in ourselves and our own strength and wisdom,

As the evening sun sets we plan for a new day. With God there is the assurance that there is always a future.